DEPARTMEN

Choosing Safety

London : HMSO

© Crown copyright 1994

Applications for reproduction should be made to HMSO

First published 1994

Second impression 1994 with corrections

ISBN 0 11 551225 X

HMSO publications are available from:

HMSO Publications Centre
(Mail, fax and telephone orders only)
PO Box 276, London SW8 5DT
Telephone orders 071-873 9090
General enquiries 071-873 0011
(queuing system in operation for both numbers)
Fax orders 071-873 8200

HMSO Bookshops
49 High Holborn, London WC1V 6HB
(counter service only)
071-873 0011 Fax 071-873 8200
258 Broad Street, Birmingham B1 2HE
021-643 3740 Fax 021-643 6510
33 Wine Street, Bristol BS1 2BQ
0272 264306 Fax 0272 294515
9-21 Princess Street, Manchester M60 8AS
061-834 7201 Fax 061-833 0634
16 Arthur Street, Belfast BT1 4GD
0232 238451 Fax 0232 235401
71 Lothian Road, Edinburgh EH3 9AZ
031-228 4181 Fax 031-229 2734

HMSO's Accredited Agents
(see Yellow Pages)

and through good booksellers

CHOOSING A SAFE AND SECURE CAR

INTRODUCTION

Two major issues for today's car buyers are safety and security. By this, we mean safety on the road and security against car crime when parked. Car manufacturers are responding by focusing more and more on safety and security features when they advertise their new models.

This booklet is intended to help car buyers use safety as the basis of their decision when they choose and buy a car. In it, you will find a great deal of advice on seat belts and child restraints because they have been proved to be crucially important to safety. The other features described are available as standard or as optional extras on many cars and offer safety benefits which could make them more desirable than some of the luxury or cosmetic items.

How you know how safe is 'safe'

Safety features for a new car are tested to comply with government regulations before the manufacturer is allowed to sell it to the public. These regulations require that before a new car can legally be put on the market, it must be shown to be able both to protect people in crashes, and also to help drivers avoid accidents in the first place.

The regulations do not restrict design but require minimum levels of safety performance. Many cars are designed to have safety performance which is clearly superior to the required minimum; some cars also have additional safety features. The regulations require minimum levels of safety performance.

Growing consumer interest in safety has played a major part in influencing car manufacturers and constantly improving regulations which in turn ensure

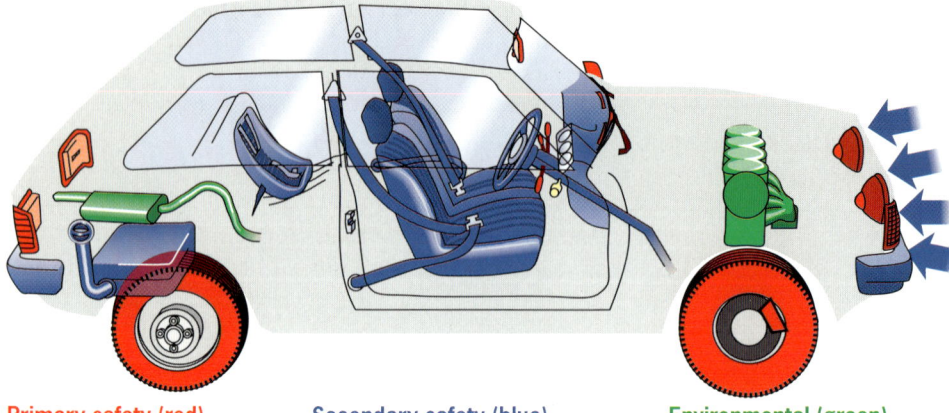

Primary safety (red)
brakes
horn
mirror
controls
defrost/demist
wipers
lights
indicators
reflectors
tyres

Secondary safety (blue)
child restraints
head restraints
steering wheel
glass
interior and exterior fittings
bumpers
frontal impact
seats and seatbelts
fuel tanks
door latches

Environmental (green)
radio interference
fuel consumption
exhaust emissions
noise

Security (yellow)
anti-theft steering locks

safer cars. It's an ongoing process that is developing all the while and this booklet is intended to play its part in bringing safety features into focus among interested car buyers.

Primary and secondary safety

There are two critical types of safety features. First, there are those that help drivers to avoid accidents and secondly, those that protect people in crashes and minimise the risk of injuries. The former are often known as 'primary' safety; the latter as 'secondary' safety features.

Good tyres and suspension, lights and brakes (with or without ABS Antilock braking) can have a dramatic influence on a drivers ability to avoid hazards and can greatly reduce the risk of an accident.

But however good these 'primary' safety features are, they cannot prevent accidents. Drivers will always remain the main cause of almost all accidents, usually involving other cars whose drivers are not at fault and who may have had no chance to take avoiding action. It is here that the car's basic design structure - the key to 'secondary' safety - plays a vital role in protection. The basic design has to take into account how structures behave and deform in real crashes and take steps to counter what happens in order to protect the occupants. Advanced computer modelling techniques make much of this possible at the design stage, allowing manufacturers to simulate crashes and predict how different structures perform and how variations in the design affect the overall performance.

Measuring safety - car by car

This booklet contains tables of car safety ratings based on the risk of driver injury. They are calculated from a study of over 100,000 real accidents involving two-car collisions.

The data comes from the police, who report on all road traffic injury accidents, and compares the proportion of drivers injured in such accidents. A relatively lower number of drivers injured per accident indicates a relatively safer car and vice versa. A fuller explanation appears with the tables starting on page 30, together with reasons why some cars do not appear in the tables.

Security against car crime

Security is also very much in the minds of car buyers since the battle against car crime has yet to be won. In 1992, the police recorded 494,000 thefts of cars. They accounted for over 11% of all recorded crime and it represents an enormous cost both to individuals and to society.

This booklet describes many of the safety and security features available in certain current models, gives advice on their effect and explains how they can be best used.

THE SAFETY FACTORS. WHAT TO LOOK FOR AND WHY

VEHICLE SIZE

When involved in an accident, a large car will on average collide with a car smaller than itself. The size and weight advantage of the large car helps protect its occupants. The other side of that coin is that this extra weight and momentum increases the risk of injury to people in the smaller car they collide with.

Larger cars also generally cost more to buy and run, use more fuel and cause more pollution than smaller cars. Those are some of the many factors to take into account when deciding what size of vehicle to buy. Others include comfort, performance, styling and, of course, what you can afford.

Our overall advice is to look at your needs and choose a general type of car first in terms of size and then weigh up the safety and security factors covered in this booklet to help you choose the best model in that selection.

DEAD STOP?

Before you think about making a choice the different stages of a collision give a good illustration as to why you should think about safety. It's a disturbing story.

Think of rattling a pebble in a tin can. Every time you change the direction your hand moves in, the pebble hits the can at the other end from the direction of travel. It's inertia that does that. Because it's inside the tin, the pebble first of all moves at the same speed as the tin. But when you change direction, because it's not fixed to the inside, it carries on moving in the same direction at the same speed until it hits the other end of the can.

When you are in a car and you run into something, the car decelerates very quickly and unless you are prevented from doing so by some form of restraint, you and your passengers, front and rear, keep on moving at roughly the same speed the car was travelling at before the impact. You are the pebble rattling in the can.

Even at 30 mph in a frontal collision, if they are not wearing a seat belt to restrain them, an average person in the front seat keeps moving forward and hits the steering wheel or windscreen and fascia with a force of three and a half tonnes.

Back seat passengers without seat belts hurtle forward and hit the back of the front seats and their passengers with equal force – equivalent to the weight of an elephant. They often clash skulls with front seat passengers which can cause serious, even fatal, injuries to both themselves and the front seat passengers.

When you're in a car that's been hit from behind it's a bit different. You and your car are suddenly forced to go forward at about the speed at which the car behind hits you.

Inertia throws your head backwards as it accelerates up to the speed of the car. If there is a head restraint, you are cushioned during this violent movement. If there is no head restraint, or if there is one, but badly adjusted, this acceleration force has to come through your neck. This force can be very high and causes what most people know as a whiplash injury. In a multiple accident you could end up being hit at both ends of your car in which case you will be at risk of suffering both sets of injuries.

Seat belts, child restraints and, lately, airbags have been proved to stop people rattling around like a pebble in a can. You know they save lives.

No one would dream of going on a giant corkscrew big dipper without demanding proper seat harnesses. Yet the forces that make that fairground ride dangerous are exactly the same as the ones acting on cars in a crash. The physical inertia due to speed can kill. So can the mental inertia that prevents people from putting on seat belts or putting children in appropriate restraints.

SEAT BELTS AND CHILD RESTRAINTS

Seat belts save lives. Wearing a seat belt is the single most important action you can take in a car to minimise your risk of injury in an accident. Since 1983, when the wearing of front seat belts was made compulsory, at least 370 deaths and 7,000 serious injuries have been prevented each year in this country alone.

The law today

If they are fitted and available, seat belts have to be used in the front of all vehicles and in the rear of cars, small minibuses and taxis (there are minor exceptions). The law does not prevent you from carrying more passengers than there are restraints, but if at all possible it should be avoided. If you have to choose who rides without a restraint, remember inertia and that heavier passengers cause greater injury to others in accidents if they are not wearing a seat belt.

It is the driver's responsibility in law to ensure that he or she and all children under the age of 14 comply with the seat belt laws in both front and rear seats. It is the legal responsibility of adult passengers to ensure they themselves comply with the seat belt laws wherever they sit.

If a child travelling in the front is under three years of age, it must be in an appropriate child restraint.

If a child restraint is fitted in the front, but not in the rear, children under three years of age must use that restraint.

An 'appropriate child restraint' mentioned here and later is a properly designed and tested baby or child seat. There are fuller descriptions of the types available later on. (See page 10)

If no child restraint is available for children aged under three years of age, it is generally safer for them to ride in a back seat wearing an adult belt rather than no restraint at all.

If an appropriate child restraint or seat belt is available in the front, but not in the rear, children between 3 and 11 and under 1.5 m in height must use the front seat restraint.

Do not allow children to stand in the rear between the two front seatbacks. With no seat belt, but just holding on between the front seats, a child in a severe accident will carry on and hit the windscreen at almost the same speed the car was travelling at when the accident happened.

Summary of the law

	Front seat	Rear seat	Who's responsible
Driver	Seat belt must be worn if fitted	–	Driver
Child under 3 years of age	Appropriate child restraint must be used	Appropriate child restraint must be used if available	Driver
Child aged 3 to 11 and under 1.5 metres (approx 5ft) in height	Appropriate child restraint must be worn if available. If not, an adult seat belt must be worn	Appropriate child restraint must be worn if available. If not, an adult seat belt must be worn if available	Driver
Child aged 12 or 13 or younger child 1.5 metres (approx 5ft) or more in height	Adult seat belt must be worn if available	Adult seat belt must be worn if available	Driver
Adult passengers	Seat belt must be worn if available	Seat belt must be worn if available	Passenger

Exemptions

There are specific exemptions on medical and other grounds. If you think you should not wear a seat belt on medical grounds, please consult your doctor. Your local Road Safety Officer will tell you about other exemptions, but the strong advice is that while seat belts can sometimes cause slight injuries, they really do prevent serious and fatal injuries. So even if exemption is available, you'll be safer wearing one if at all possible.

FRONT SEAT BELTS

Seat belt retractors (inertia reels)

When a vehicle is slowed by hard braking or in a crash, inertia works for you and locks the seat belt retractors automatically. These 'inertia reels' have a second mechanism that locks when the shoulder belt itself is suddenly jerked. You can test for this by tugging sharply on the belt. A good habit to get into when you prepare to drive off is to pull the belt tight across the body and tug the diagonal belt sharply to lock the reel.

Pre-tensioners and webbing grabbers

It is important to minimise the amount of slack belt. In a severe impact, the loose belt can allow enough movement for you to hit the steering wheel or dashboard. Pre-tensioners and/or belt webbing grabbers can reduce the chance of this happening, so increasing your chance of surviving a severe accident.

Pre-tensioners tighten belts during the first milliseconds of a crash, before you start to move. Webbing grabbers clamp the belt webbing just outside the reel. These two features, separately or preferably together, reduce the likelihood of your moving forward far enough to be injured.

Shoulder belt height adjusters allow the diagonal belt to be moved to provide a comfortable fit for people of varying heights. Adjust to the position where the diagonal belt is comfortable, but not in contact with the neck, ideally midway across your shoulder.

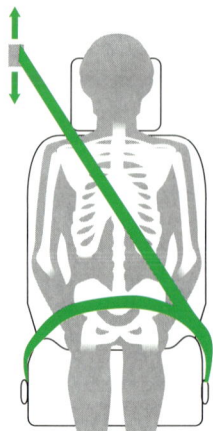
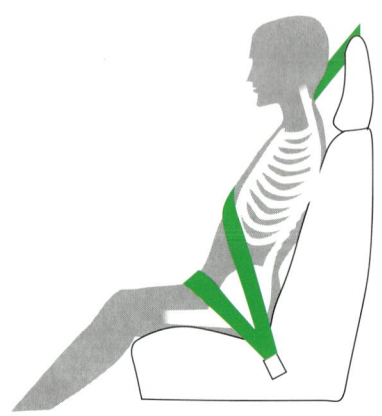

Rear belts and lap belts

The compelling reasons to use rear seat belts - apart from legal requirements - are described in the section 'Dead Stop' on page 4.

All cars built after October 1981 have anchorage points for fitting rear seat belts. You can buy rear seat belts at most car accessory shops and garages. When in doubt, have them professionally fitted.

Since April 1987, all new cars have had rear seat belts fitted as standard equipment. When looking at rear seat belts, remember that lap belts are not as effective as lap-and-diagonal belts. However, they are still much safer than not wearing a belt at all.

Lap belts rarely have automatic retractors, so they should be adjusted to be reasonably tight. This is because any slackness allows movement forward and in an accident, your movement forward and abrupt stop against the belt applies a sudden load to the spine, which could possibly cause serious injury.

When wearing a lap belt, it should fit low and snug across the pelvis, not over the stomach

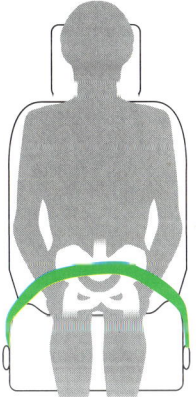
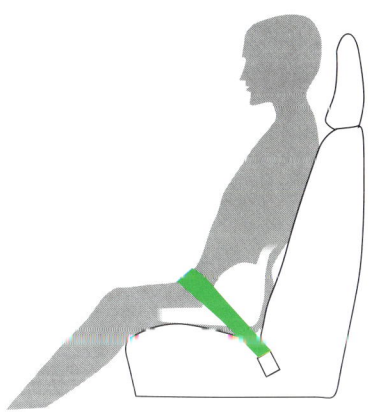

CHILD RESTRAINTS

The risks

Every year in the UK, some 500 children are killed or seriously injured in car accidents because they are not properly restrained. The greatest risk to a child's life from the age of one is an accident. One in five of the children killed in traffic accidents is a passenger in a car, where the most common sort of accident is a head-on collision resulting in the injuries already described. These deaths and injuries can be avoided by making sure your children are restrained every time they travel in a car. It's much safer.

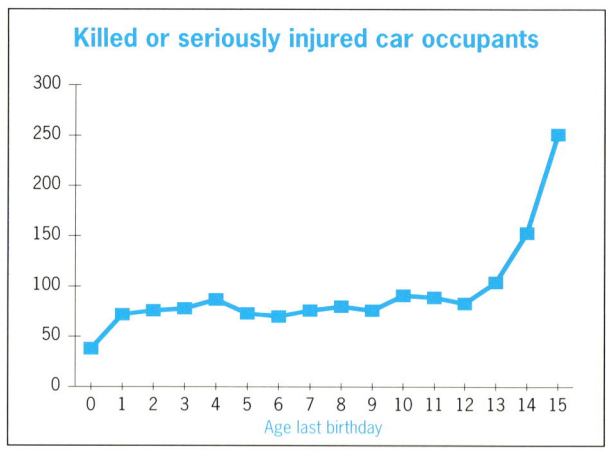

Never put a baby between yourself and the seat belt you are wearing. In a crash, the weight of your body would move forward until the seat belt stopped you. At 30 mph, if you're of average size, you would exert a force of 3 1/2 tonnes on your baby's body. It would be squashed between you and the belt and possibly crushed to death.

Choosing child restraints
Restraints are available in a wide variety of types - baby seats, child seats, booster seats and booster cushions.

The appropriate restraint depends on the weight, size and age of your child. For a very young child the safest type of restraint is the baby seat, also called a rear-facing infant carrier. You can use a baby seat for babies from birth until they weigh about 10 kgs (22 lbs), usually at about 9 months.

Carrycots
Carrycots with restraint straps are not designed to withstand the considerable forces generated in an accident. A baby seat is safer and more convenient than a carrycot, although doctors may occasionally advise the use of carrycots, eg for premature babies. The best advice is that carrycots should be used only if the alternative is to travel with your child without any type of restraint at all.

Never put your baby in the luggage space of hatchbacks or estate cars except in a restraint specifically designed for that purpose.

Baby seats
Baby seats can be fitted in the front or rear seat of a car using the adult lap-and-diagonal seat belt. If the baby seat is convenient to use and carry you are more likely to use it on every journey. It is slightly safer to use the seat in the rear than the front of the car. Rear facing seats provide very high levels of protection and are generally safer than forward facing seats.

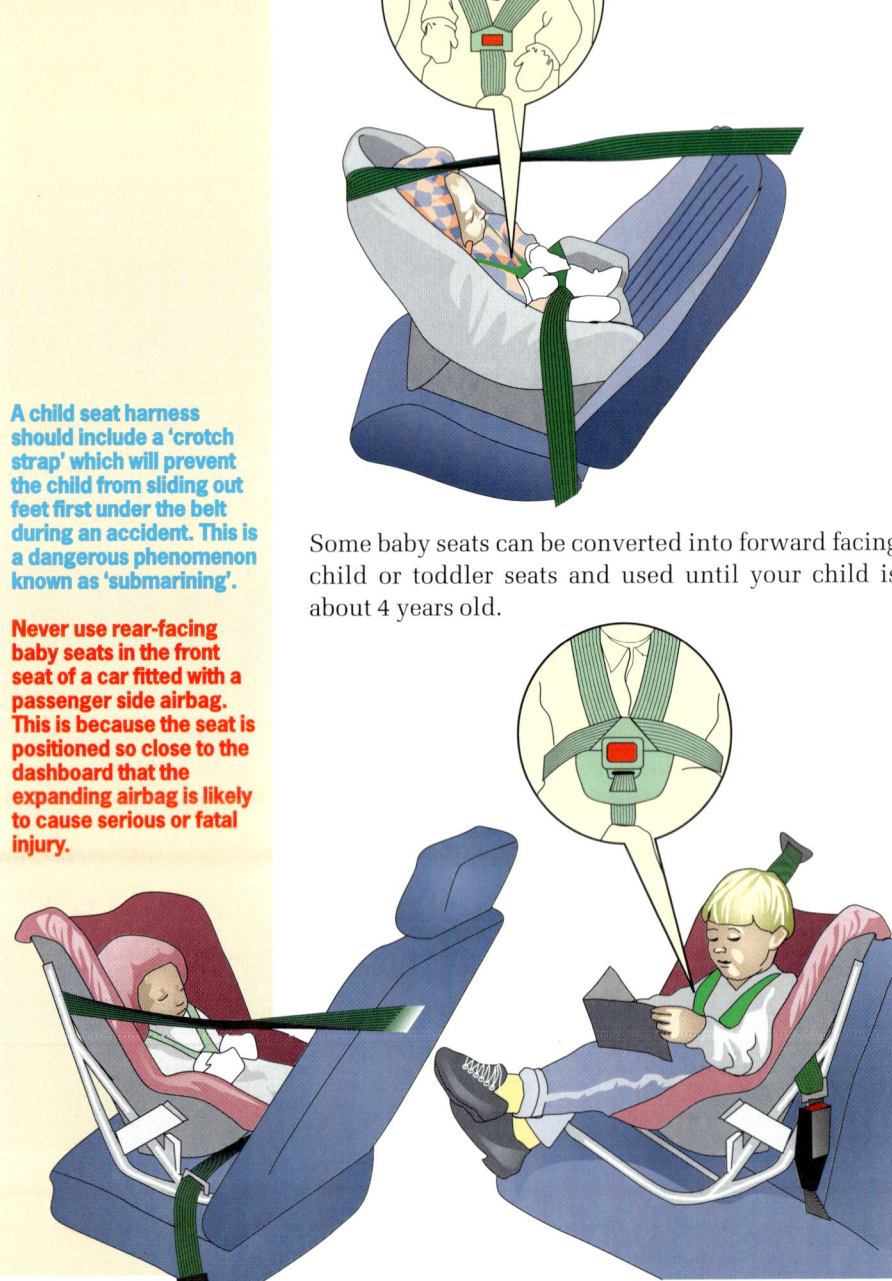

A child seat harness should include a 'crotch strap' which will prevent the child from sliding out feet first under the belt during an accident. This is a dangerous phenomenon known as 'submarining'.

Never use rear-facing baby seats in the front seat of a car fitted with a passenger side airbag. This is because the seat is positioned so close to the dashboard that the expanding airbag is likely to cause serious or fatal injury.

Some baby seats can be converted into forward facing child or toddler seats and used until your child is about 4 years old.

Child seats

Some child seats for children of about 9 kg to 18 kg (about 4 years) are in the form of a 'booster seat'. Some use the adult seat belt to restrain the child, while others use the belt to secure a frame seat which has its own integral harness.

Booster seats are generally easier to install correctly, provided a lap and diagonal seat belt is available. The frame seat has the advantage of having a harness specifically designed for a child in that age group.

Booster cushions

These are used for children who are too large for a child seat and are designed to adapt the positioning of the child to make the adult seat belt suitable for use. They are recommended for children from around 4 years up to 10 years and are very effective at modifying the fit of an adult belt to suit their smaller bodies.

Favour a booster cushion with a guide strap to improve the position of the shoulder belt

STEERING WHEELS AND COLUMNS

The risks

Unless their car is fitted with an airbag, drivers are most likely to be injured in an accident by hitting their face or head on the steering wheel or column. When choosing a safer car, look at the design of the steering wheel. It is critically important and should allow a good depth of padding on any hard parts in its construction. Avoid steering wheels which do not have substantial padding in the centre or on the rim, and have hard objects such as switches where your head or face might hit.

Good

- Cross section showing metal positioned away from face
- Nut set deep into hub
- Stiff but flexible padding
- No switches or hard badges
- Large diameter hub pod
- Thick padding on spokes

NB Some deep hub steering wheels still have the nut close to the face

Bad

- Hard cover, little or no padding
- No depth available to set nut deep into hub
- Small hub
- Little padding on stiff bakelite or wooden rim

NB A slim hub cannot have the nut set deep into it

It is not possible for non-experts to assess the effectiveness of energy-absorbing steering columns, but guidance on this and other 'secondary' safety aspects of some popular models is available in consumer magazines.

Distance from the steering wheel

A suitably comfortable driving position is an essential factor to bear in mind when choosing a new car. As a driver, you can help prevent injury to yourself by adjusting seat and steering wheel positions.

Obviously, you need to reach and work the pedals to have full control of the brakes in particular - but you also need to be as far as practical from the steering wheel. Most instructors recommend a comfortable arm's length distance and not to drive leaning towards the steering wheel with your arms fully bent. Keeping away from the steering wheel and column reduces the risk of impact injuries to your face and head in an accident.

AIRBAGS

Airbags operate in moderate to severe frontal collisions. Crash sensors send signals to airbag inflators which fill the bags in a fraction of a second with harmless gas. Full inflation occurs in less than 1/20th of a second, faster than the blink of an eye. The bags fill and begin to deflate instantly, cushioning the impact.

Accident experience in the USA shows that airbags save lives and prevent many serious injuries, especially to the head and face, which belts alone would not have prevented.

However, airbags are designed to work in conjunction with seat belts and should not be thought of as a substitute for belts. An airbag will not protect you - because it's not designed to do so - in lower severity frontal impacts, in impacts from the side or rear, or in rollovers. Seat belts should always be used, even when airbags are fitted – it's the law as well.

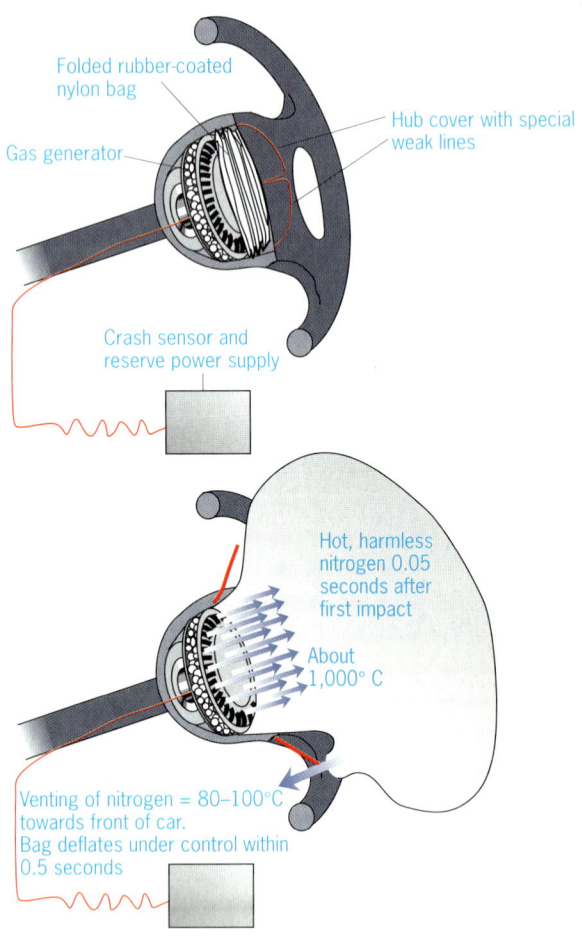

Since last year, many new cars have had driver's side airbags fitted as standard equipment. Even some of the smallest cars are starting to get airbags as well. It is a fact that seat belts plus airbags do provide the best possible protection in a frontal crash. Therefore, on the surface it makes sense when you are choosing a car to favour one fitted with a driver's side airbag, but an airbag alone will not make a car safe.

Some new cars are now becoming available with front passenger airbags. There is too little data to draw firm statistical conclusions, but scientific judgement suggests that their benefits may be limited.

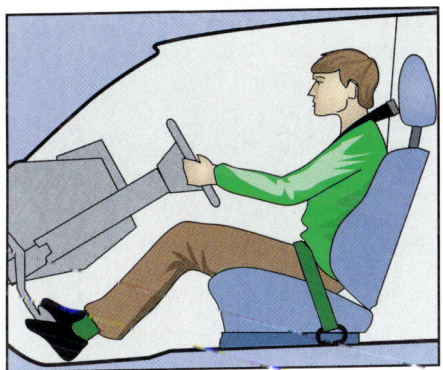

1. Normal driving position at point of impact

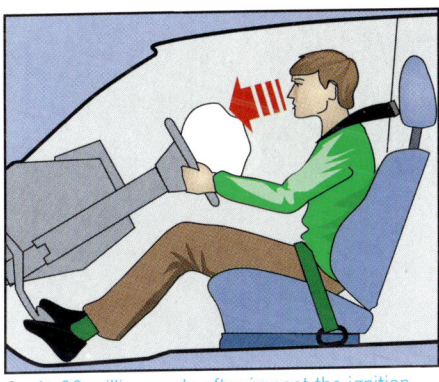

2. At 20 milliseconds after impact the ignition capsule activates and the airbag breaks through the steering wheel cover. This is also the time the driver begins to move forward.

3. 50 milliseconds and the bag is fully inflated. The driver's face hits the cushion.

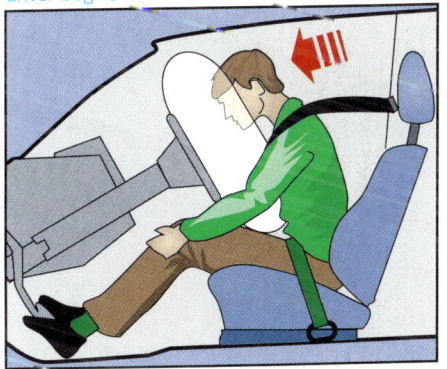

4. 80 milliseconds. The full weight of the driver's head has been cushioned and the bag begins to collapse.

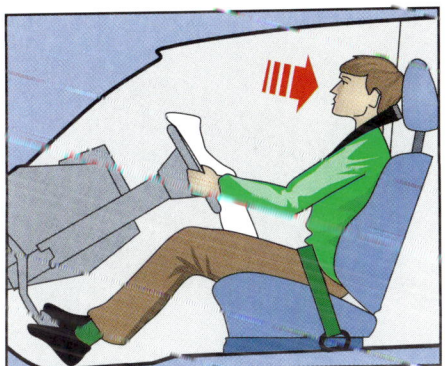

5. 150 milliseconds. Driver has returned to his original position and the bag has emptied. A good reference to this time scale: it takes 200 milliseconds for the human eye to blink.

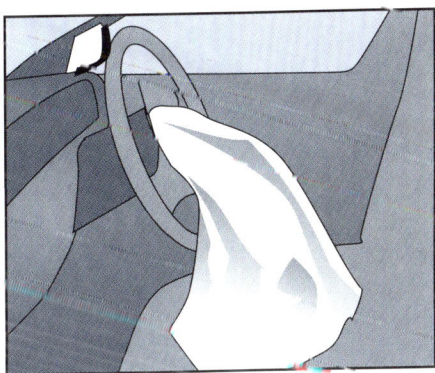

6. When an airbag has deployed the deflated bag will remain outside the steering wheel cover.

Full size or Eurobag?

Advertisements for cars with airbags may refer to 'Eurobags' and 'full size bags'. The smaller Eurobag is designed primarily to prevent face and head injuries when the seat belt is worn. Protection from chest

injuries from hitting the steering wheel is by the diagonal part of the seat belt.

The full size airbag is based on US designs. There is, as yet, insufficient data to judge which is the safer when used in conjunction with a seatbelt, as it should be.

Airbag dangers

Airbags and their control systems are maintenance free and should never be tampered with - they contain explosives with the potential to cause injury.

Do not fit a rear-facing child seat in the front passenger seat of a car with a passenger side airbag, because the seat (and child) are too close to the rapidly-inflating airbag. Two-seater cars with passenger airbags are not suitable for carrying a child up to about nine months as an appropriate child seat is rear-facing and incompatible with the airbag. Similarly front seat passengers should never put their feet on the dashboard in case the airbag is activated.

The speed and force of airbag inflation may occasionally cause minor injuries such as abrasions and slight burns, but this slight risk is far outweighed by the benefits. The risk of injury from the airbag itself is reduced by driving in a position that doesn't put your face close to the steering wheel.

◆ HEAD RESTRAINTS

When you are in a car hit from behind, the sudden movement forward makes your head jerk backwards. This is known as whiplash and head restraints are designed to prevent it and the injuries it can cause. Head restraints are less common for rear seats than for front seats; but for rear passengers - tall ones in particular - they are an important additional safety feature in rear end crashes.

Injuries like whiplash which may seem relatively slight, can in fact turn out to be very long-term and painful, but are relatively easy to prevent by correct use of the head restraint, so it makes sense to choose a vehicle with good head restraints.

Head restraints essentially come in two types: adjustable and fixed. Adjustable restraints may have to be positioned manually, behind occupants' heads, for protection.

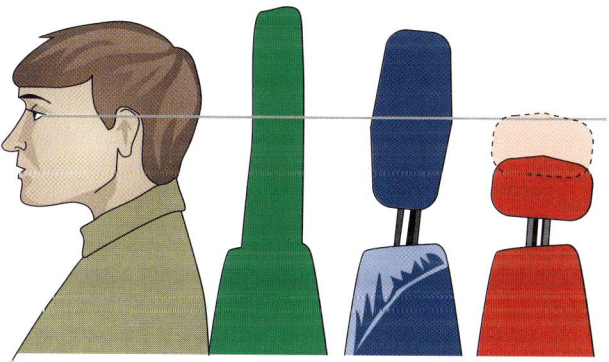

The good adjustable restraint shown above would protect most people, even in the 'down' position. But the one on the right, if in the lowest position (as it usually is), would protect only the shortest people. Therefore the best choice would be a good adjustable or fixed head restraint.

SIDE IMPACT

It is difficult to achieve adequate protection against side impact, because there is very little structure in a door between you and the vehicle hitting yours. The way to protect you is complicated and involves physically moving you out of the way before being hit by the car coming into you.

Favour a car with padded door trim panels and armrests positioned forward of your chest when seated in your normal travelling position. The simple addition of a 'side impact bar' to strengthen the door will not necessarily improve your chances of escaping serious internal injury in a full side impact, although it may help in front or glancing impacts by reducing the other car's intrusion into your passenger compartment.

BULL BARS

Bull bars or nudge bars are often seen on 4WD off-road vehicles but are also fitted to vans. People who fit them may not be aware of the increased danger to pedestrians and cyclists.

Many vehicles have smooth shapes, helping to reduce pedestrian injuries. Bull bars make them worse. In crashes with other vehicles the bull bar can interfere with the intended crash protection. In light impacts the bull bar can increase the amount of damage; it is pushed into the bodywork across the full width of the vehicle whereas the damage might have been restricted to one side.

Insurance companies should be notified of the alteration to the vehicle. In some cases they have acted against the policy holder where an injury or accident damage was made worse by a bull bar.

When a pedestrian is hit by a car the risk of serious or fatal injury is high. The thin bodywork of a car front does bend and provide some padding. A steel bull bar does not. Adults may suffer more serious leg, knee and pelvic injuries with an increased risk of internal injuries from bull bars. Children are at an even greater risk because the top bar might make direct contact with their head. If this happens survival chances are limited. Whilst at 20 mph many children could survive an impact by a car, in theory a vehicle with a bull bar could kill at 10 mph.

Think twice before buying a bull bar. If you already have one, why not consider removing it?

LOAD RESTRAINT

In the same way that back seat passengers should wear seat belts - remember the elephant in the back of the head analogy - you should always try to strap heavy loads down to prevent them hurtling forward in a frontal accident. The 'parcel shelf' is a very inappropriate name, because in an accident, items on it, like packages, umbrellas or even dogs (and it has happened!) can cause serious injuries in this way.

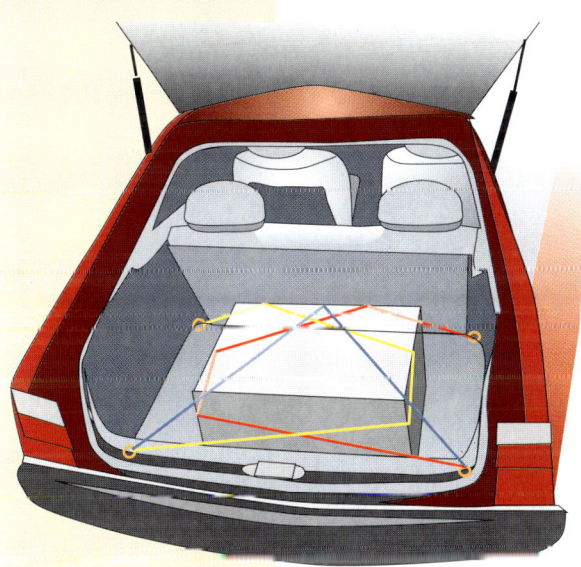

The boots of most modern cars are quite large; but people who regularly wish to transport moderately heavy objects of over 25kg such as a sack of potatoes, should look for cars fitted with tie down eyes, which are small loops attached to the floor or side panels: few manufacturers already fit them. The inside of most car boots is lined with carpet and therefore it is not possible to fasten down heavy objects

Tie-down eyes are of great benefit to people using a car for business purposes, to carry samples, merchandise or service equipment. The folding seats in hatchbacks and estates, especially those with split seats, are rarely strong enough to hold back heavy loads in a heavy frontal accident. Saloons with non folding seats are more likely to prevent this dangerous shifting of heavy loads.

Some safety-conscious manufacturers are fitting strong folding seat structures. These can not only restrain the load but can also support a three-point mounting for the centre seat belt. These cars can easily be recognised by the rear seat centre belt having both lap and diagonal straps.

ACCIDENT AVOIDANCE

Primary Safety
The secondary safety features that help you survive an accident are good, but it's even better to avoid accidents altogether. Features that help drivers avoid accidents are known as 'primary' safety.

Many 'primary' safety features are difficult to see just by looking at a car. For example, all cars must have a back-up braking circuit to ensure that the car can still stop if there is any problem with the main brakes. This type of 'primary' safety is built in to cars to comply with regulations. However, there are other good 'primary' safety features which can be detected by looking at and sitting in a car.

Visibility
Sit in the driver's seat. Can you see all you need to out of the front window or do the front pillars block the view? Is it easy to see when reversing or do the rear pillars restrict lines of sight? Are there enough mirrors and do they give a good view or have blind spots; can you see the corners of the car or at least gauge accurately where they are? Can you see clearly through front and rear screens or are there reflections? Heavy tinting, stickers and most cracks are against the law and could cause a car to fail its MOT. Good all round visibility is a 'primary' safety feature of critical importance.

Controls

Sit in the driver's seat. Can all the important dials be seen? Try the minor controls to see if they are easy to reach and use without needing to take your eyes off the road or move in your seat. Work the heating and demisting features and try to judge if they will do their job well. Think about cooling and fresh air ventilation especially face level vents which help prevent motorway fatigue.

Visibility and controls can be assessed initially while sitting in a stationary car, but are best judged as elements of primary safety by using them during a test drive.

Antilock braking system (ABS)

ABS prevents a vehicle's wheels from skidding by applying and releasing the brakes automatically, many times a second. What they are doing is 'pumping' the brakes - applying them to the point of skidding, then releasing them. In doing so, ABS should allow drivers to maintain full steering in an emergency stop in all road conditions.

On wet and slippery surfaces, you have to apply ordinary brakes very gently to prevent skidding. ABS brakes modulate the pressure to suit the conditions.

The overriding advantage of ABS is that it allows you to steer around an obstacle whilst still braking as hard as you can.

ABS brakes are of great benefit in emergencies, but should not be provoked into operation in normal driving. ABS will not improve your car's braking performance on gravel or snow. They will not reduce braking distances on dry surfaces and should not be relied on to do so on any surface. You must not try to 'pump' ABS brakes yourself because pumping prevents effective operation.

Cars with ABS will have a dashboard light which lights up when you start the car to show that certain checks of the ABS are being made. If it stays lit a fault has been detected and the car should not be driven until repaired.

Traction control system (TCS)

In slippery conditions, such as ice or snow, it is often difficult to accelerate without the wheels spinning. Traction control prevents wheelspin by automatically controlling the accelerator or the brakes to produce a smooth take-up of drive. Traction control is an aid to primary safety by helping to keep the car under control.

Four wheel drive (4WD)

In slippery conditions, or on off-road surfaces, it is helpful if all the wheels can be used to get the power from the engine onto the road. 4WD allows all the wheels to drive and improves primary safety by making the most of the grip that the tyres have on the road.

4WD is available both on the rugged off-road types of vehicle typified by the Range Rover, and on more conventional cars. Your choice of 4WD or not is governed very much by your needs and the uses to which you will put your vehicle.

Stability

Stability is difficult to judge and depends on how well the car maker has balanced the need for stability when accelerating, braking and cornering using such things as suitable tyres, suspension and weight distribution. Your choice of car will depend on what you want to use it for. This will influence the shape of the car. However, if a car is low to the ground with a wheel at each corner, it is likely to be more stable than one with a short wheelbase, a narrow track and a high centre of gravity. Looking for a car with 'primary' safety stability features might even make you rethink your needs or influence the way you drive your chosen car.

LIGHTS

It is important that the lights on your vehicle are working properly and that they are clean. You need to see at night and, importantly, others must be able to see you, your brake lights and indicators to know what you intend to do.

Make sure that your dipped headlights are correctly adjusted. When your vehicle is loaded or towing a trailer, the headlamps ideally require adjusting; on some cars this can be done from the drivers seat. Badly adjusted lights can mean that you are either dazzling other road users or you have a poor view of the road ahead. If in doubt ask your garage to reset your lights.

Use of fog lights

Do not switch on front or rear fog lights just because it's dark or raining. It is illegal to use them unless visibility is 'seriously reduced' - generally less than 100 metres. Remember to switch them off at all other times because they don't make you more visible, all they do is dazzle the driver behind, and because of that can actually cause an accident.

Stop lights

Research has shown that separate (as opposed to combined) stop lights and tail lights - as on some current models - can help following drivers respond more quickly to brake signals. There are similar advantages in having a third stop light located away from the other rear lights, usually mounted centrally and fairly high up.

MAINTENANCE

'Primary' safety features help avoid accidents but only if they work. All the features mentioned here will help to avoid accidents but again only if they are maintained in proper working order.

As you look at each feature while choosing your car, try to judge how difficult it may be to maintain. Choose cars where the features need no maintenance, are automatically checked or adjusted, or where maintenance is easy.

PROTECTING YOUR VEHICLE

Car theft

Door and steering locks fitted by the car manufacturers should not be relied on to deter a thief. There are numerous add-on alarm systems and immobilisers which can substantially improve the security of your car (motorcycle, van or truck). Modern cars are now more likely to have car alarms and immobilisers fitted as standard.

Locks

In all thefts from closed vehicles, and in nearly all thefts of vehicles, it is necessary for the thief first to gain entry. Entry is usually gained through a door, a window or the boot. Door locks which conform to British Standard (BS) AU 209 Part 1A give a good level of basic security. They will prevent the door being easily forced open and the internal linkages being activated simply with a coat hanger to release the latch mechanisms.

Central locking

Central locking systems which conform to BS AU 209 Part 5A include locks which meet the requirements of Part 1A and ensure that all the doors lock when the driver's door is locked. This should reduce the risk of any door being left unlocked. This is especially convenient if you often have several passengers as all four doors will usually be unlocked.

Deadlocks

In recent years some cars have been fitted with deadlocks (sometimes called double locks or super locks). The effect of these is that even if a thief breaks a window the door cannot be unlocked using the interior controls. Such cars are less attractive to joy riders and thieves as they usually have to climb in and out through a broken window. Deadlocking systems can be approved to BS AU 209 Part 6.

Immobilisers

Since 1972 new cars have been required to be fitted with an 'immobiliser', usually in the form of a steering column lock. These operate when the key is removed, although the steering wheel should be turned until a click is heard to engage a column lock. Your car can be made more secure by using an additional immobiliser. These are essentially of two types: mechanical immobilisers, which prevent the driving of the car; and electronic immobilisers, which affect the operation of the engine.

Additional mechanical immobilisers

Additional mechanical immobilisers generally have a heavy lock and prevent the use of one or more essential controls. Early ones connected the brake pedal to the steering wheel; many recent models lock a bar to the steering wheel, preventing it being rotated. Others lock the gear stick in a fixed position or connect the handbrake to the gear lever. These are not suitable for cars with a screwed-in gear stick if it can be unscrewed and re-inserted free of the immobiliser. Buyers should be careful when choosing a mechanical immobiliser and should always ensure that it is removed fully and stored safely before driving away.

Additional electronic immobilisers

Additional electronic immobilisers generally prevent a car from starting. Simple ones only break the starter motor circuit, and can be bypassed by a determined thief. The more complex, effective and expensive electronic immobilisers interact with the engine ignition system and prevent it being started or running. Immobilisers which can be set or come into effect when the engine is running or the vehicle is moving are dangerous and should be avoided.

Alarm systems

An alarm which sounds if a door lock is forced or a window broken can be an effective deterrent but only if the owner is within earshot.

To be effective alarm systems must only sound following an 'attack' on a vehicle, they must not suffer from false alarms. Alarm systems which conform to the British Standard are of proven quality and have good reliability under test conditions.

Tracking recovery systems

For cars of high value or at high risk of being stolen it might be worth considering a hi-tech electronic tracking system which helps the police to recover the car if it is stolen. A very determined thief may be able to bypass an immobiliser or simply use a truck to carry the vehicle to a workshop. Cars stolen in this way are difficult to recover. A tracking system will direct the police to where the car is hidden and though it will not prevent it being stolen it will greatly improve the chance of it being recovered. The cost of such a system has to be considered in relation to the value of the car in question.

Security marking

A cheap method of discouraging car thieves is to have the registration number etched onto the glass. This will not deter the joy rider but will make it difficult for a thief to simply change the number plates and sell it as a different car.

Benefits of added security

The 1991 Home Office leaflet on car theft looked at the effect on the theft rate of fitting additional security measures. The chart below shows the change for three high-risk 'volume' cars, the newer models of which have been fitted, by their manufacturers, with significantly improved security features. The models - Vauxhall's Cavalier and Ford's Escort and Fiesta - are all less likely to be stolen with the security features than were the older models without them.

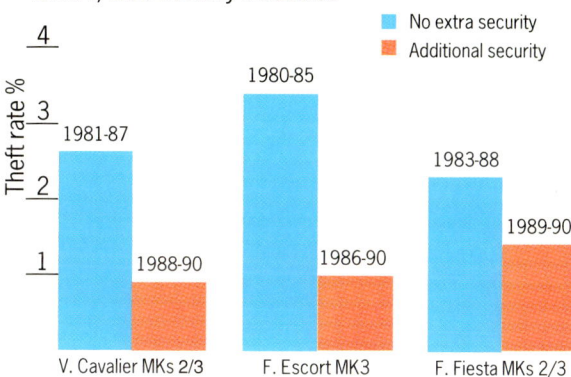

Theft Rates in Volume Ranges
Before/after security measures

NB. In each case the fall in the theft rate is still highly significant after allowing for the effects of vehicle age on theft.

Parking

The security features described above offer no absolute guarantee against car theft so you should always park in the safest possible place. Don't give a criminal an open invitation. When you leave your car unattended –

> Choose a busy and well lit area, preferably where you can see your vehicle.

> Use attended car parks where possible.

> If you are parking at home, use a garage if you have one and lock it. Otherwise, choose your space carefully.

Securing

> Ensure that the steering lock is engaged.

> Switch on, or fit, any additional security devices, particularly immobilisers.

> Always lock every door and close every window, including the boot and sunroof (unless you leave a pet in the car).

30 | MINI AND SUPERMINI CARS (up to 150 ins / 380 cms long)

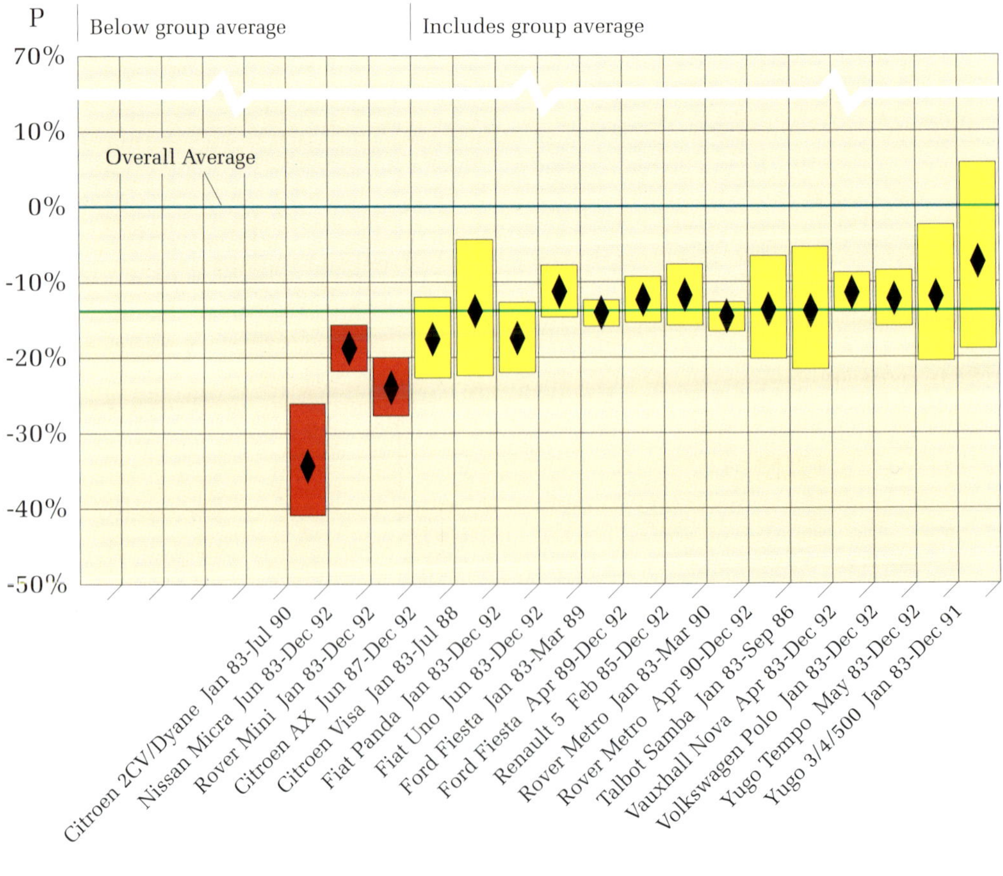

P | Below group average | Includes group average

- 70%
- 10%

Overall Average

- 0%
- -10%
- -20%
- -30%
- -40%
- -50%

Citroen 2CV/Dyane Jan 83-Jul 90
Nissan Micra Jun 83-Dec 92
Rover Mini Jan 83-Dec 92
Citroen AX Jun 87-Dec 92
Citroen Visa Jan 83-Jul 88
Fiat Panda Jan 83-Dec 92
Fiat Uno Jun 83-Dec 92
Ford Fiesta Jan 83-Mar 89
Ford Fiesta Apr 89-Dec 92
Renault 5 Feb 85-Dec 92
Rover Metro Jan 83-Mar 90
Rover Metro Apr 90-Dec 92
Talbot Samba Jan 83-Sep 86
Vauxhall Nova Apr 83-Dec 92
Volkswagen Polo Jan 83-Dec 92
Yugo Tempo May 83-Dec 92
Yugo 3/4/500 Jan 83-Dec 91

HOW TO READ THE CHARTS

Example is based on Yugo Tempo May 83-Dec 92 which is in the Mini and super mini cars chart.
1. Protection value of the average Mini and supermini car shown by green line.
2. Protection value of the overall average car shown by blue line.
3. Protection value best estimate for Tempo shown by the diamond ♦ 12% below the overall average car.
4. Most likely upper and lower limits of protection value for Tempo shown by yellow bar.
5. The colour of the bar indicates whether the car can confidently be classified as above, or below the average protection value for the particular group.
6. Protection value P is based on the risk of injury to drivers:
a=risk of injury to drivers in the particular car
b=risk of injury to drivers in the overall average car
P=(b-a)x 100%
       b
7. For each size of car, we have given the bars three different colours. For models whose protection rating is completely below the average for that size of car, the bars are red; for those completely above the average the bars are blue; and those within the average for their size have yellow bars. For each colour we have shown the models in alphabetical order, as the variability of the best estimate of their protection values does not allow us to predict precisely the order that they should be in.

Above group average

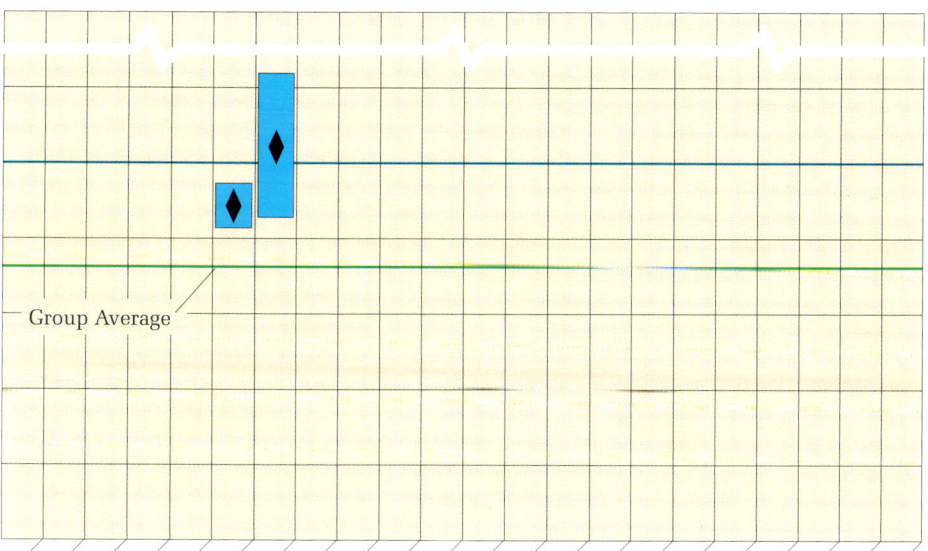

32 **LOWER MEDIUM CARS** (up to about 165 ins / 420 cms long)

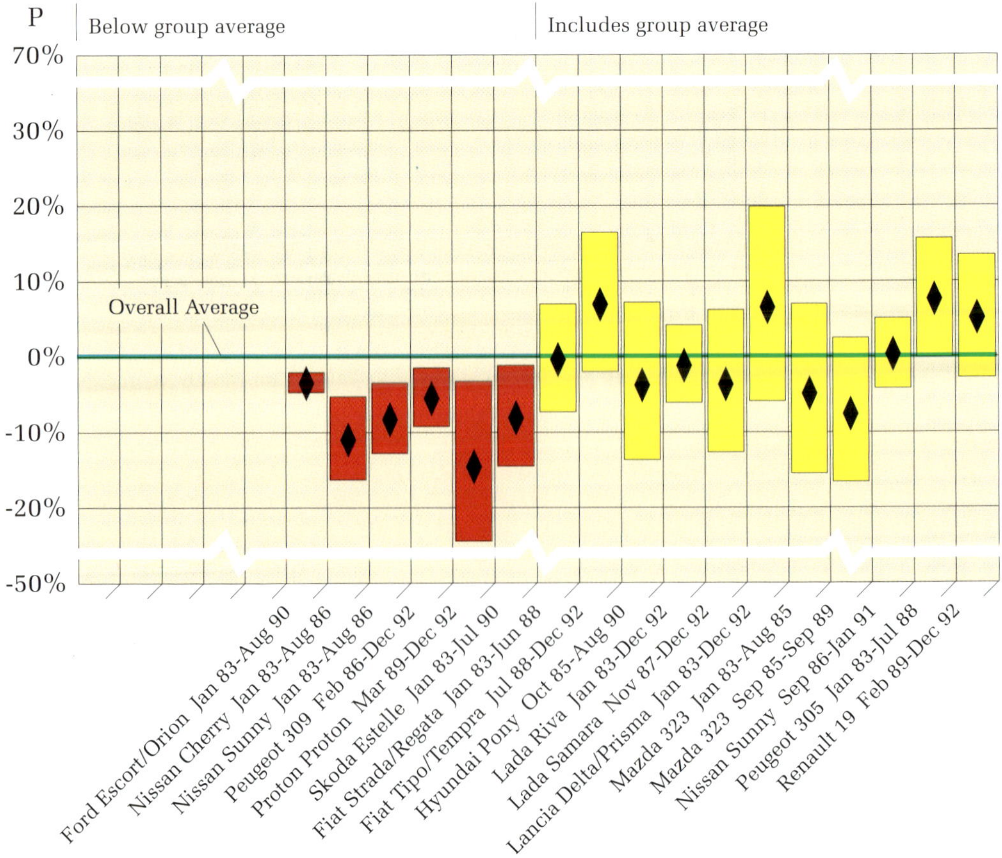

P
- 70%
- 30%
- 20%
- 10%
- 0% Overall Average
- -10%
- -20%
- -50%

Below group average | Includes group average

Ford Escort/Orion Jan 83-Aug 90
Nissan Cherry Jan 83-Aug 86
Nissan Sunny Jan 83-Aug 86
Peugeot 309 Feb 86-Dec 92
Proton Proton Mar 89-Dec 92
Skoda Estelle Jan 83-Jul 90
Fiat Strada/Regata Jan 83-Jun 88
Fiat Tipo/Tempra Jul 88-Dec 92
Hyundai Pony Oct 85-Aug 90
Lada Riva Jan 83-Dec 92
Lada Samara Nov 87-Dec 92
Lancia Delta/Prisma Jan 83-Dec 92
Mazda 323 Jan 83-Aug 85
Mazda 323 Sep 85-Sep 89
Nissan Sunny Sep 86-Jan 91
Peugeot 305 Jan 83-Jul 88
Renault 19 Feb 89-Dec 92

HOW TO READ THE CHARTS

Example is based on Seat Ibiza/Malaga Oct 85-Dec 92 which is in the Lower medium cars chart.
1. Protection value of the average Lower medium car shown by green line.
2. Protection value of the overall average car shown by blue line.
3. Protection value best estimate for Seat Ibiza/Malaga shown by the diamond ♦ 1.8% above the overall average car.
4. Most likely upper and lower limits of protection value for Seat Ibiza/Malaga shown by yellow bar.
5. The colour of the bar indicates whether the car can confidently be classified as above, or below the average protection value for the particular group.
6. Protection value P is based on the risk of injury to drivers:
a=risk of injury to drivers in the particular car
b=risk of injury to drivers in the overall average car
$P = \frac{(b-a)}{b} \times 100\%$

7. For each size of car, we have given the bars three different colours. For models whose protection rating is completely below the average for that size of car, the bars are red; for those completely above the average the bars are blue; and those within the average for their size have yellow bars. For each colour we have shown the models in alphabetical order, as the variability of the best estimate of their protection values does not allow us to predict precisely the order that they should be in.

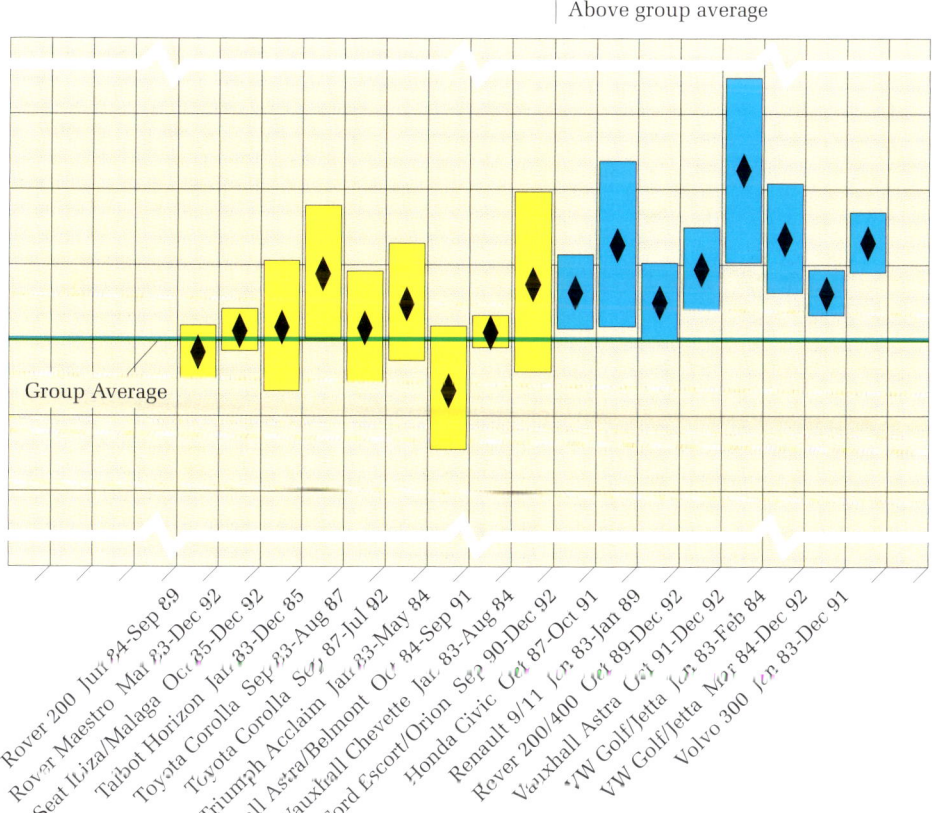

34 UPPER MEDIUM CARS (up to 180 ins / 455 cms long)

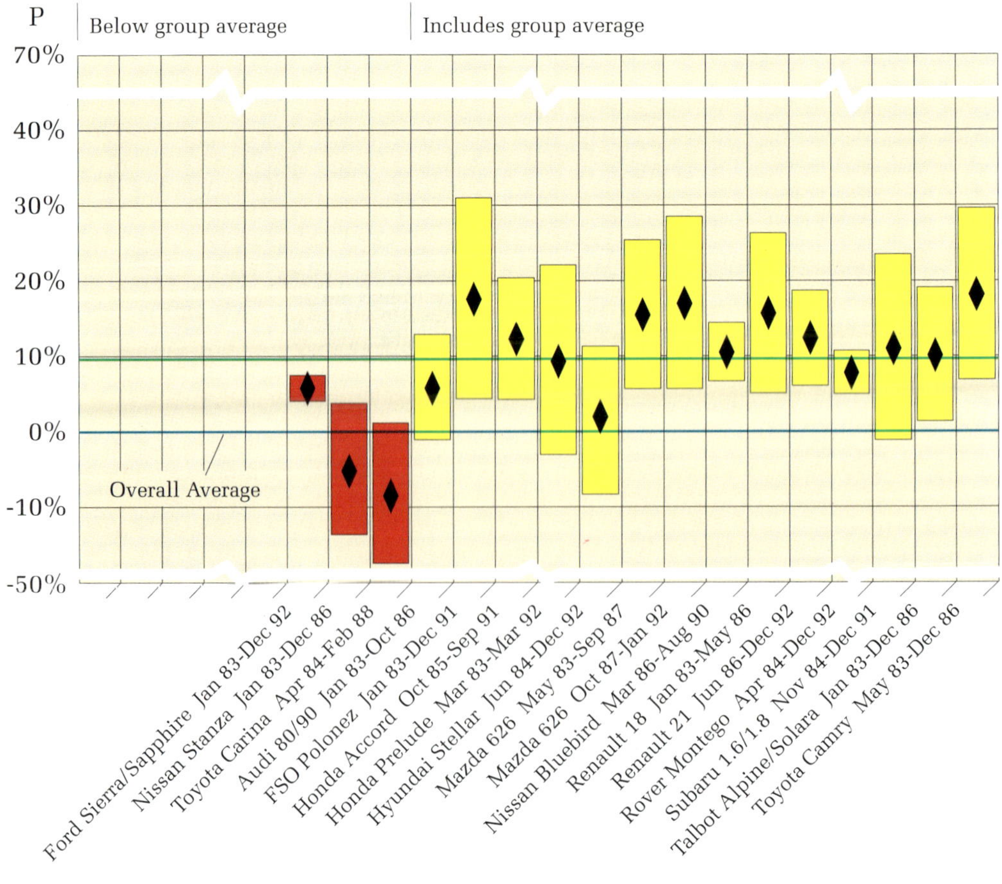

P

| | Below group average | Includes group average |

70%
40%
30%
20%
10%
0%
-10%
-50%

Overall Average

Ford Sierra/Sapphire Jan 83-Dec 92
Nissan Stanza Jan 83-Dec 86
Toyota Carina Apr 84-Feb 88
Audi 80/90 Jan 83-Oct 86
FSO Polonez Jan 83-Dec 91
Honda Accord Oct 85-Sep 91
Honda Prelude Mar 83-Mar 92
Hyundai Stellar Jun 84-Dec 92
Mazda 626 May 83-Sep 87
Mazda 626 Oct 87-Jan 92
Nissan Bluebird Mar 86-Aug 90
Renault 18 Jan 83-May 86
Renault 21 Jun 86-Dec 92
Rover Montego Apr 84-Dec 92
Subaru 1.6/1.8 Nov 84-Dec 91
Talbot Alpine/Solara Jan 83-Dec 86
Toyota Camry May 83-Dec 86

HOW TO READ THE CHARTS

Example is based on Vauxhall Cavalier Jan 83-Sep 88 which is in the Upper medium cars chart.

1. Protection value of the average Upper medium car shown by green line.
2. Protection value of the overall average car shown by blue line.
3. Protection value best estimate for Vauxhall Cavalier shown by the diamond ♦ 8.6% above the overall average car.
4. Most likely upper and lower limits of protection value for Vauxhall Cavalier shown by yellow bar.
5. The colour of the bar indicates whether the car can confidently be classified as above, or below the average protection value for the particular group.
6. Protection value P is based on the risk of injury to drivers:
a=risk of injury to drivers in the particular car
b=risk of injury to drivers in the overall average car
$P = \frac{(b-a)}{b} \times 100\%$

7. For each size of car, we have given the bars three different colours. For models whose protection rating is completely below the average for that size of car, the bars are red; for those completely above the average the bars are blue; and those within the average for their size have yellow bars. For each colour we have shown the models in alphabetical order, as the variability of the best estimate of their protection values does not allow us to predict precisely the order that they should be in.

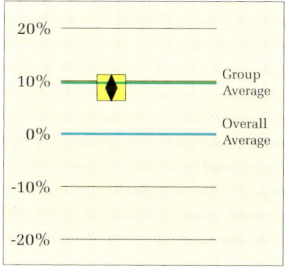

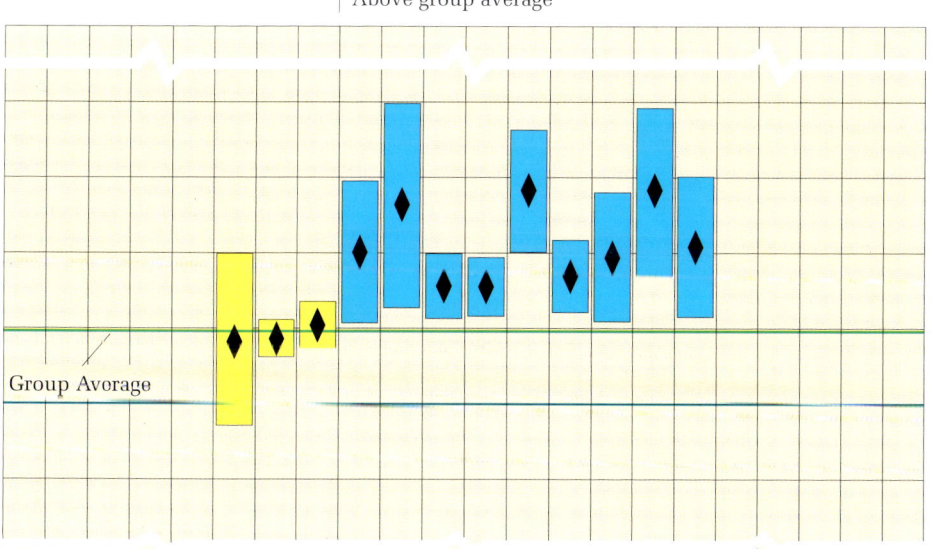

EXECUTIVE AND LUXURY CARS (over 180 ins / 455 cms long)

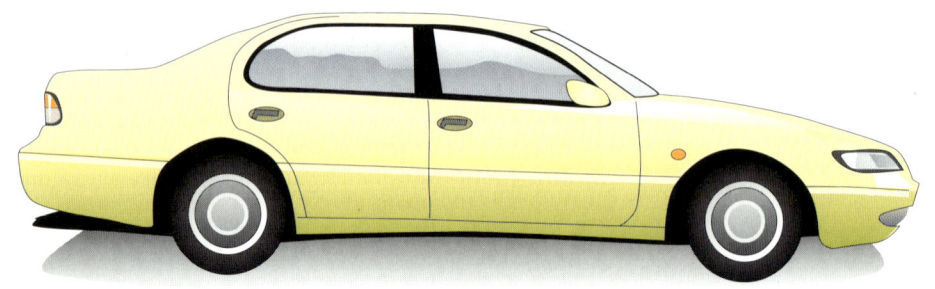

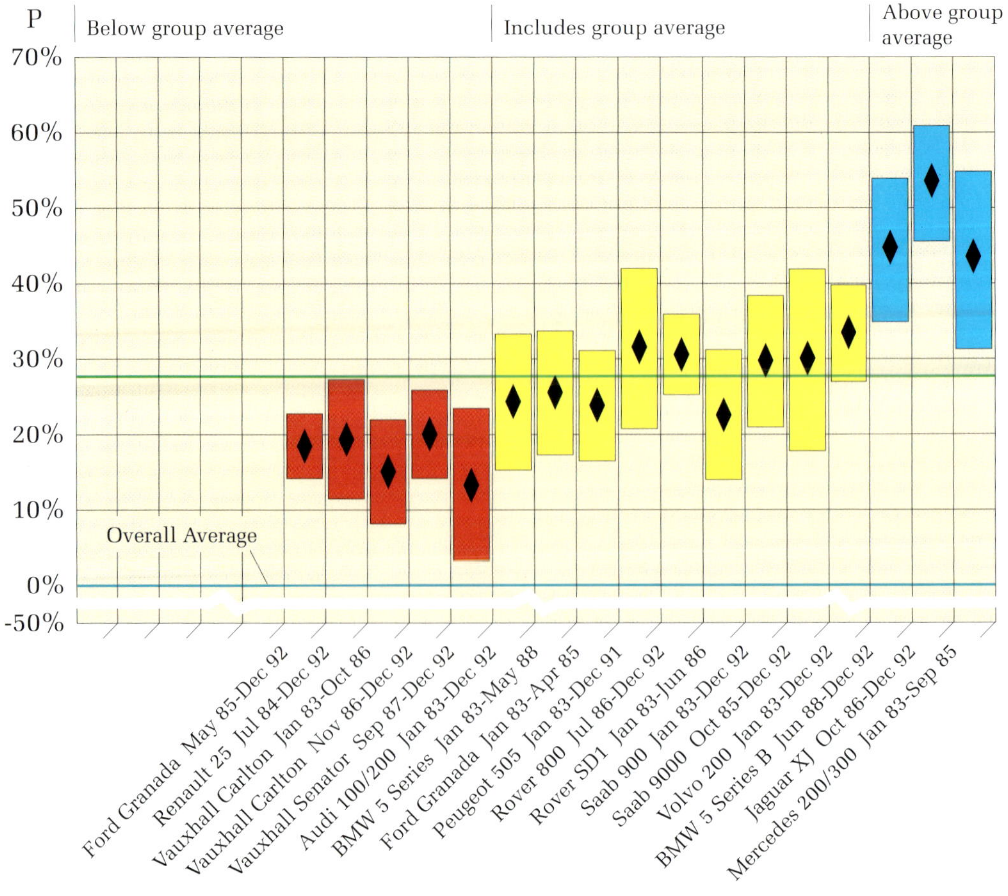
P
Below group average
Includes group average
Above group average
70%
60%
50%
40%
30%
20%
10%
0%
-50%
Overall Average
Ford Granada May 85-Dec 92
Renault 25 Jul 84-Dec 92
Vauxhall Carlton Jan 83-Oct 86
Vauxhall Carlton Nov 86-Dec 92
Vauxhall Senator Sep 87-Dec 92
Audi 100/200 Jan 83-Dec 92
BMW 5 Series Jan 83-May 88
Ford Granada Jan 83-Apr 85
Peugeot 505 Jan 83-Dec 91
Rover 800 Jul 86-Dec 92
Rover SD1 Jan 83-Jun 86
Saab 900 Jan 83-Dec 92
Saab 9000 Oct 85-Dec 92
Volvo 200 Jan 83-Dec 92
BMW 5 Series B Jun 88-Dec 92
Jaguar XJ Oct 86-Dec 92
Mercedes 200/300 Jan 83-Sep 85

HOW TO READ THE CHARTS

Example is based on Rover 800 July 86-Dec 92 which is in the Executive and luxury cars chart.
1. Protection value of the average Executive and luxury car shown by green line.
2. Protection value of the overall average car shown by blue line.
3. Protection value best estimate for Rover 800 shown by the diamond ♦ 30.6% above the overall average car.
4. Most likely upper and lower limits of protection value for Rover 800 shown by yellow bar.
5. The colour of the bar indicates whether the car can confidently be classified as above, or below the average protection value for the particular group.
6. Protection value P is based on the risk of injury to drivers:
a=risk of injury to drivers in the particular car
b=risk of injury to drivers in the overall average car
$$P = \frac{(b-a)}{b} \times 100\%$$

7. For each size of car, we have given the bars three different colours. For models whose protection rating is completely below the average for that size of car, the bars are red; for those completely above the average the bars are blue; and those within the average for their size have yellow bars. For each colour we have shown the models in alphabetical order, as the variability of the best estimate of their protection values does not allow us to predict precisely the order that they should be in.

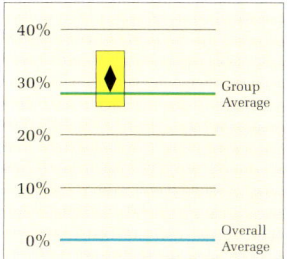

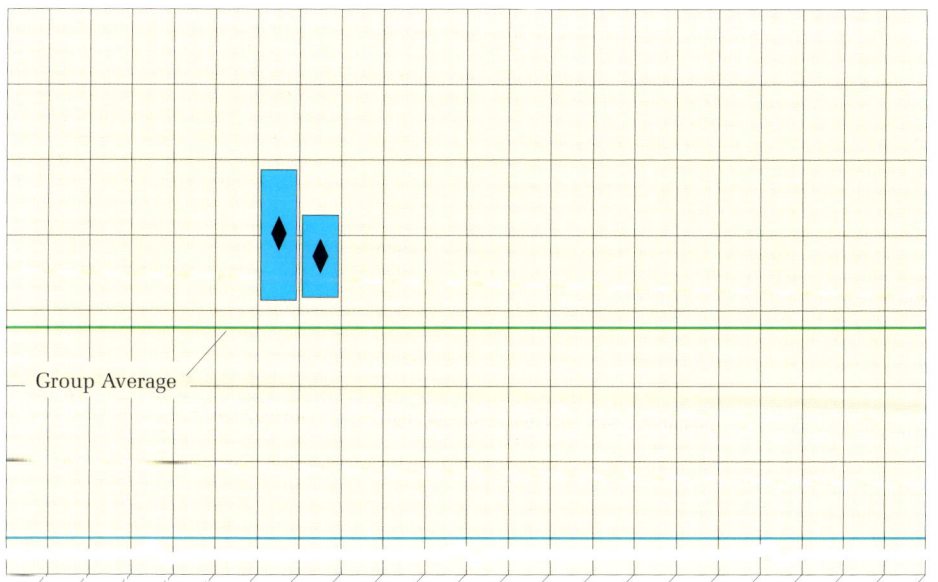

Where do the facts come from?

The data comes from the police who report on all road traffic injury accidents. The ratings in this leaflet are based on reported personal injury road accidents data relating to accidents between two cars. For each model the starting point of the comparison is the proportion of drivers in the model who are injured in such accidents: a relatively low proportion indicates a relatively safe car, and a higher proportion a less safe car.

However, the risk of driver injury depends not only on the safety features of a particular model, but also on the type of accident and driver, which may differ in different car models.

The relative car driver injury rates are therefore adjusted in an attempt to compensate for the distinctions due to different driver behaviour and accident types in particular models of car, so that comparisons more closely reflect those safety features of the car which directly influence the risk of injury to the driver.

Details of these corrections and an explanation on how these are derived can be found in *Cars: Make and Model: The risk of Driver Injury and Car Accident Rates in Great Britain: 1992*.

Your car is not in the tables?

We are very careful not to base our advice on unreliable statistics. A model of car has to be involved in sufficient accidents for a statistically reliable judgement to be made. Until there is sufficient data we do not publish the results. For some models that are not numerous we may never have sufficient data to say how safe they are. Remember that new types of cars produced since 1992 cannot figure in these results.

Printed in the United Kingdom for HMSO
Dd 298086, C350, 7/94